THE LITTLE SCENTED LIBRARY·

LAVENDER

·JOANNA SHEEN·

SIMON AND SCHUSTER

NEW YORK·LONDON·TORONTO·SYDNEY·TOKYO·SINGAPORE

A DORLING KINDERSLEY BOOK

SIMON AND SCHUSTER
SIMON & SCHUSTER BUILDING, ROCKEFELLER CENTER
1230 AVENUE OF THE AMERICAS, NEW YORK, NY 10020

FIRST PUBLISHED IN GREAT BRITAIN IN 1991 BY DORLING KINDERSLEY PUBLISHERS LIMITED.
9 HENRIETTA STREET, LONDON WC2E 8PS

PRINTED IN HONG KONG

10 9 8 7 6 5 4 3 2 1

2

LIBRARY OF CONGRESS CATALOGING-IN-PUBLICATION DATA
THE LITTLE SCENTED LIBRARY.
P. CM.
INCLUDES INDEX
CONTENTS: LAVENDER / JOANNA SHEEN -- SCENTED GIFTS / VALERIE JANITCH --
POTPOURRI / MALCOLM HILLIER -- ROSES / MALCOLM HILLIER.
ISBN 0-671-73416-4. -- ISBN 0-671-73417-2. -- ISBN 0-671-73415-6. -- ISBN 0-671-73418-0
1. POTPOURRIS (SCENTED FLORAL MIXTURES) 2. AROMATIC PLANTS. 3. FLOWER
ARRANGEMENT. I SHEEN, JOANNA. II. JANITCH, VALERIE. III. HILLIER, MALCOLM.
TT899.4.L68 1991
745.92--DC20   80-19646

ISBN 0-671-73416-4

CONTENTS

INTRODUCTION

A LUXURIOUS HAZE of purple lavender is one of life's more simple pleasures. Along with the heady scents of old-fashioned roses, honeysuckle and freshly mown grass, the sweet fragrance of lavender transports me immediately to the dreamy summers of my childhood.

Lavender has long been popular. In England both Queen Elizabeth and Queen Victoria used it as a preserve and perfume, and tradition has it that on Midsummer's Eve, revellers throw bunches of lavender on to bonfires as part of the ritual celebrations. Lavender is also an important healing herb and is still used today in aromatherapy to ease stress and tension.

Dried lavender is a main ingredient in many potpourri recipes and is frequently used to fill sachets, cushions and herb pillows; lavender can even be used in cooking. Fresh lavender adds a decorative element to flower displays, and its scent perfumes any bouquet. Lavender oil can be used in moisturizers, skin toners, creams, perfumes and bath oils.

There are many ways to enjoy the wonderful scent of lavender. When its flowering season is over, let the fragrance of lavender linger on with the ideas suggested in this little book.

THE SCENT OF LAVENDER

*L*AVENDER OIL IS AN ESSENTIAL OIL often used in aromatherapy massage to help relieve aches and tension. It is first mixed with a vegetable oil – a carrier – in the ratio of six drops of essential oil to every 2 oz (50 g) of carrier oil. Suitable carrier oils include: soybean, sesame, sunflower and safflower oil. Other essential oils frequently used in aromatherapy include lemon and rosemary oils.

Carrier oil

Vetiver oil

Lavender oil

LAVENDER OIL
Lavender oil is distilled from the plant and is then mixed with a carrier oil for use in aromatherapy massage.

Lemon

SOOTHING SOLUTIONS

To help you relax after a stressful day, simply add a few drops of straight lavender and vetiver oil to a hot bath; or try gently massaging the stomach area with a mixture of lavender oil and a carrier oil. For aching feet that have done a lot of walking, a restorative ten-minute soak in a bowl of water containing several drops each of lavender and juniper oils works wonders. For fast, soothing relief from sunburn, add 20 drops of lavender and chamomile oils to a cool bath.

MEDICINAL REMEDIES

Lavender has long had a reputation as a reliever of headaches. Add 12 drops of lavender oil to 4 oz (100 g) of carrier oil and massage gently around the temples and the base of the skull. It is also thought to help restore the balance of the nervous system; use 6 drops each of cypress and lavender oils in 4 oz (100 g) carrier oil; massage the stomach area in a counterclockwise direction with your right hand. Lavender oil will also soothe insect bites and stings.

Carrier oil

Lavender

Lavender oil

7

Rosemary

USING LAVENDER

*L*AVENDER HAS MANY DECORATIVE and aromatic uses inside the home. One simple yet stunning idea is to pack a plain basket or pot with several large bunches of fresh lavender and display it in a prominent position in the hall or living room. Less extravagant but no less charming arrangements can be created using small sprigs of lavender in combination with other small, scented flowers.

To preserve lavender's summery scent throughout the winter, hang bunches up to dry and then fill sachets and cushions with the dried lavender.

BASKET DISPLAY

*This breathtaking display will form
the centerpiece in any room. Fill a
basket with dried floral foam and
insert bunches of lavender into this
until the basket virtually overflows.
Add ribbon bows to finish.*

FRESH DISPLAYS

*L*AVENDER IS AN IDEAL FLOWER to display in fresh-
flower arrangements – it looks pretty in any
size and shape of display, whether large or
small, and with virtually all types of plant material,
but it is particularly successful with old-fashioned,
cottage-garden flowers. A collection of herbal
flowers and aromatic plants, for example, makes
a wonderfully subtle country-style arrangement.
For a more formal effect, try combining
sprigs of lavender with old-fashioned
roses. The heady perfume of the
lavender flowers will add to
the appeal of any display.
If you are going to use
lavender in a large
arrangement, you
will need to wire
several stems
together to
create a
stronger
effect.

LAVENDER & ROSES

This stunning table centerpiece consists of a mass of pink and mauve roses, freesias and lavender surrounding two candles scented with lilac. To make this display, attach some floral foam to a piece of cork for the base. Insert the candles into holders and push them into the foam, then insert the foliage to create the overall shape. Fill out the shape with roses and freesias, and finally insert the lavender sprigs. Subtle fragrances are lovely for a table centerpiece, but take care not to overpower your food with large arrangements of strongly scented flowers, or with heavy aromas such as hyacinth.

OLD-FASHIONED POSIES

W ITH ITS BEAUTIFUL COLOR and pungent scent, fresh lavender makes an ideal ingredient for an old-fashioned posy. Posies are traditionally composed of scented flowers and they make perfect gifts. Arrange a few stems of lavender with other fragrant flowers such as roses, freesias, and sweet peas, or with sweetly scented herbs such as sage and rosemary. To complete, tie with a ribbon.

SIMPLE ROSE POSY
A ring of lavender and white baby's breath surrounds a delicate, pink rose. Two satin ribbons complete the posy.

SUMMERY BOUQUET

Lavender and baby's breath flowers, interspersed with freesias, encircle a tight bunch of roses. Sage leaves and lady's mantle make a textured, scented border.

13

DRIED DISPLAYS

*L*AVENDER IS AN IDEAL FLOWER to use in a dried-flower arrangement as it dries so easily, and it has the added appeal of retaining its wonderfully rich scent. To air-dry lavender, simply hang a bunch upside-down in a warm, dry area for about a week. For a stunning display, group bunches of dried lavender in a rustic container, or try combining it with dried peonies, roses, and herbs for a complex arrangement.

SIMPLE & EFFECTIVE
The beauty of this flower arrangement (below) is in its simplicity. A cluster of dried peach-colored roses nestles in a small glass dish, surrounded by a fragrant frill of lavender and a few achillea flower heads.

FLOWERS IN A TEACUP
This pretty little teacup (above) makes the perfect setting for an arrangement of dried lavender, red spray carnations, and achillea flowers.

LAVENDER BASKET
A simple but sumptuous display of vivid purple lavender looks perfect in a rustic woven basket. Cream ribbon bows add contrasting color and a stylish finishing touch.

15

Tussie Mussies

POSIES OF FRESH or dried flowers, or tussie mussies as they were known in the past, make a special token of affection or a thoughtful way to say thank you. Whether they convey a traditional message using the language of flowers, or please the recipient with their colors and fragrance, tussie mussies always make lovely gifts.

CHILD'S ROSE POSY
This posy is made with lavender, masterwort and roses.

FORMAL BOUQUET
The loops of satin ribbon add style to this large posy of scented flowers.

SUBTLE COLOR SCHEME
Lavender is predominant in this posy of purple, yellow and pale green flowers.

17

LAVENDER IN A BAG
A fine net bag filled with fragrant, dried lavender forms the center of this pretty tussie mussie, and is surrounded by circles of Sweet William flowers and golden-colored carnations.

LAVENDER BUNDLES

*L*AVENDER BUNDLES are dried stems of lavender woven together with ribbon. They are easy to make, requiring nothing more than a little care, patience and nimble fingers. Collect the lavender just as it begins to flower so that the flower oils are at their strongest and cut the stems as long as possible. You need 11 or 13 stems for each bundle.

MAKING A LAVENDER BUNDLE

1 Trim the stems of the lavender and tie them all together in a neat bunch, just below the flower heads, with a long piece of narrow ribbon.

2 Gently and carefully bend each stalk back over the flower heads to form a cage around the flowers. If any of the stalks snap, just begin again.

3 Attach a tiny safety pin to the end of the ribbon then weave the ribbon in and out of the stalks, starting at the top and continuing until you reach the base of the flower heads.

4 Wind the ribbon around the stalks of the lavender and tie it in a bow. Trim the stalks to neaten.

COMPLETED BUNDLES

Place the finished lavender bundles in a warm, dark place, such as an airing cupboard, to dry completely before using. Then place them on your dressing table or tuck them in a drawer and enjoy their fragrance.

LAVENDER & LINEN

*L*AVENDER HAS A WONDERFUL FRAGRANCE for scenting all your linens, smelling crisp yet wonderfully warm and clean. Sheets and table linen scented with lavender have been enjoyed by people for literally hundreds of years. Lavender bundles provide both an attractive and practical way to tuck lavender into drawers and linen cupboards. They can also be placed between stored woollen blankets.

LAVENDER BUNDLES
Place bundles of lavender in a handkerchief drawer, or between sheets in a linen cupboard.

SWEET-SCENTED NAPKINS

Store your linen table napkins by rolling them up with a lavender bundle and securing with a napkin ring. This will give them a fresh, sweet fragrance when you come to use them at the table.

POTPOURRIS

*M*AKING YOUR OWN MIX of potpourri is fun and so rewarding, but also quite easy. All recipes use different combinations of fragrant flowers, but lavender is one of the most popular. Add it to pungent herbs, exotic spices, fixatives and aromatic essential oils.

LAVENDER MIX
Combine lavender flowers and stalks with dried rue leaves and add 6 drops of lavender oil. Decorate with shells.

LAVENDER &
ROSE MIX

*Mix 4 cups (1 liter)
dried roses and
alchemilla with 2 oz
(50 g) lavender; add
1 oz (25 g) ground
orris root, 3 drops of
lavender oil, and 2
drops of rose oil.*

EXOTIC POTPOURRIS

*W*ITH THE MANY ESSENTIAL oils available today, it is simple to create more exotic potpourris. Add a few drops of patchouli oil or ylang-ylang oil for a heady fragrance, or mix in some scented woods, such as sandalwood and cedarwood for a musky perfume. In the potpourri mix below, a spicy perfume is achieved by using cinnamon, cloves and nutmegs as well as lavender and orange oils.

SPICY MIX
Mix cornflowers, lavender, spices, citrus peel, ground orris root and essential oils.

OLD-FASHIONED ROSE MIX

Mix together 4 cups (1 liter) of dark rose petals and lavender flowers, then add 2 drops each of rose oil and cinnamon oil, and 1 oz (25 g) ground orris root for a fragrant pot-pourri mix (above).

SCENTED BOX

Create an unusual potpourri (left) by displaying aromatic bay leaves, star anise, cinnamon and lavender in a compartmented box. Add a few drops of essential oil to strengthen their individual fragrances.

MAKING A SACHET

L AVENDER'S CRISP FRAGRANCE has long been popular in scenting laundry. In the past, women draped newly washed linen over aromatic lavender bushes to add a lovely perfume as it dried. Sweet bags or sachets of lavender and other herbs can be tucked between sheets in the linen cupboard to keep the laundry smelling fresh, or tied with ribbon loops and hung from a radiator or drawer handle to perfume the room with the sweet, fresh smell of lavender.

MAKING A
LAVENDER SACHET

1 Cut a piece of fabric about 8 x 6 in (20 x 15 cm) and a length of lace 8 in (20 cm) long.

2 Turn under a small hem on one of the long sides and attach the lace to this. Fold the material in half, right sides together, and sew across the bottom and open side. Turn the sachet right-side out and fill it two-thirds full with lavender. Tie a satin ribbon bow around the sachet to seal it.

COMPLEMENTARY COLORS
Scented sachets made in pretty matching fabric look attractive displayed together. Tie on extra ribbon loops to hang the sachets from a radiator or coat hanger, or place them flat in a drawer or on the dressing table.

PILLOWS

H ERBAL PILLOWS have such a wonderful scent that even if they are not guaranteed to be sleep-inducing, their relaxing fragrance can be appreciated at any time of the day. Stuff your pillows and cushions with fiberfill and then add dried lavender, on its own or mixed with other herbs.

DRAWER FRESHENERS
Place small sachets in drawers for a refreshing lavender scent.

PRETTY &
PRACTICAL

*Frills of cream lace
and tiny ribbon bows
decorate this pretty
lavender pillow. For ease
of washing, the lavender
has been inserted in a
removable separate sachet
and sewn to the top of the
pillow. If the scent of the
lavender begins to fade
over time, revive it by
gently bruising the
lavender or by adding a
few drops of essential oil.*

LAVENDER SLEEP PILLOW
*This sleep pillow (opposite) is made in
a fabric to match the lavender filling.*

BATH BAGS

*E*NJOY THE SOOTHING FRAGRANCE of lavender in the bathroom with lavender bath bags and potpourri. Bath bags are easy to make and can be reused several times. Cut a piece of muslin about 7 in (17 cm) square, and fill the middle with lavender flowers. Gather the edges together and tie them in a bundle. Hang the bag from the hot tap with a ribbon.

RELAXING BATH BAGS
Loop a bath bag over the hot tap of a bath and enjoy the soothing fragrance released by the hot water.

SEASIDE POTPOURRI

A lavender potpourri mix, containing pink rosebuds, lavender, and tiny seashells, looks pretty displayed in a clear glass jar. Remove the lid from time to time to allow the delicious flowery fragrance of the potpourri to waft through the steamy air of the bathroom.

BATH OILS & WATERS

*I*N DAYS GONE BY, large houses had a still-room where the mistress of the house concocted all her aromatic and herbal remedies. Strongly scented lavender makes wonderfully fragrant waters and essences that are perfect for giving as presents. Spend some time searching for just the right bottle for your preparations – antique shops and markets often yield treasures. If you wish to heighten the lavender color, add a little natural food coloring.

SKIN TONER
Mix together 1 cup (250 ml) of lavender flowers and ¹/4 cup (60 ml) of ethyl alcohol in a screw-top jar (far left). Leave to steep for six days. Strain and decant.

FACIAL RINSE
Add 7 drops of lavender oil to 2 cups (500 ml) of noncarbonated mineral water (left).

LAVENDER MOISTURIZER

This concoction (below) makes your skin feel wonderfully smooth and the fragrance is heavenly. In a blender, combine 3 tablespoons each of gum arabic powder and almond oil, and 15 to 20 drops of lavender oil. Turn the blender on to high speed and, while the ingredients are mixing, slowly pour in 1 cup (250 ml) of noncarbonated mineral water to produce a creamy emulsion. Transfer the moisturizer to a pretty pot and store in the refrigerator.

LAVENDER & ROSE SPRINKLING WATER

Pour 1 cup (250 ml) of rose water into a bottle (left). Add 3 sprigs of fresh lavender and 3 sprigs of fresh rosemary. Seal the bottle and leave it in a warm place, such as an airing cupboard, for a couple of weeks for the scents to infuse. Then strain and decant into a decorative bottle. Sprinkle this water on to linen as you iron it for a lovely, lingering perfume.

BATH OIL

In a jar (right), mix 1/2 cup (125 ml) almond oil and 5 tablespoons of lavender oil. Cover; leave for two weeks.

PERFUMED SOAPS

OAPS OFTEN HAVE AN ATTRACTIVE FRAGRANCE of their own but, if you like, you can perfume plain, unscented soaps with a refreshing scent of lavender. Simply place the soaps in a container of lavender potpourri and leave for a week or two. As well as looking charming in the bathroom, they look good as guest soaps.

SOAPS IN A BASKET
A charming basket decorated with roses makes a delightful container for lavender soaps, which are embedded in lavender flowers.

POTPOURRI NESTS

Pretty pink guest soaps nestle in a bed of richly scented eucalyptus, peony and lavender potpourri inside two old-fashioned glass dishes.

BATHROOM FEATURE

Pretty glass dishes are particularly attractive as containers for potpourri and soap, as you can see the colorful ingredients through the sides, adding to the effect of the display. Another decorative idea for a container would be to use a rustic basket lined with a lace-edged handkerchief. Decorate all the visible sides of your potpourri with beautifully shaped and colorful petals, so that it really looks as wonderful as it smells!

A TASTE OF LAVENDER

*A*LTHOUGH MAINLY PRODUCED FOR ITS PERFUME, lavender lends a delicious and elusive flavor to food, both sweet and savory. In cooked dishes, add one or two leaf shoots to casseroles and remove before serving. A sprig of lavender shoots enhances roast lamb in a similar way to rosemary. Apple jelly made with a sprig of lavender is especially successful with pork and lamb, while lavender-flavored mustard provides a delicious accompaniment to beef and veal. Fresh lavender shoots add a pungent flavor to summer salads.

Lavender also blends well with sweet dishes. Try adding the flowers to ice-creams, sorbets and even fresh fruit salads for refreshing and tasty desserts. For a truly delicious dessert, stew apples with a few lavender flowers and serve with whipped cream.

LAVENDER MUSTARD
Mix 1 part dried lavender with 10 parts English mustard.

Dried lavender

LAVENDER HONEY
Heat 2 cups (225 g) honey with ¹/₂ cup (150 ml) lavender for 10 minutes. Strain into a jar.

LAVENDER OIL
Insert 2 or 3 sprigs of fresh lavender in a bottle of virgin olive oil and leave to mature in the sun for two weeks. It adds a fresh taste to salads.

LAVENDER VINEGARS
Insert several sprigs of fresh lavender into a bottle of white wine vinegar or cider vinegar, then seal the bottle and leave it for two to three weeks in a warm or sunny spot. Use the vinegars to add a sharp flavor to savory sauces, salad dressings and lavender jellies.

37

TEA TIME

*L*AVENDER TEA HAS LONG BEEN considered a remedy for headaches caused by tension and nervous problems. Queen Elizabeth I always had lavender on hand for tea and other medicinal uses. Lavender is a more unusual ingredient in biscuits and cakes but can add a delicious tang to a sweet biscuit. Various recipes can be adapted to incorporate lavender flowers, but a plain, buttery shortbread recipe seems to work particularly well. Lavender jelly spread on brown bread or scones is also a delicious tea-time treat, or try lavender and rosemary or lavender and apple preserve. Experiment with the amount of lavender you use until you find the right level.

LAVENDER TEA

Pour a cupful of boiling water over a tablespoon of dried lavender flowers and steep for about three to four minutes. Serve the tea with honey, or a slice of lemon for a more tangy flavor.

LAVENDER BISCUITS

*Cream ¹/₂ cup (125 g) butter with
¹/₂ cup (125g) sugar and add 1
beaten egg. Mix in 1 tablespoon of
dried lavender flowers and 1 cup
(150 g) self-raising flour. Place the
mixture in small heaps on a greased
baking tray and bake at 350°F for
about 15 to 20 minutes or until the
biscuits are golden brown in color.*

Index

ACKNOWLEDGMENTS

The author *would like to thank* DAVID CHRISTIE *of Jersey Lavender Farm,*
St Brelade, Jersey, Channel Islands,
for his helpful information and supplies of fresh lavender;
and MANDY HOLMES *and* DIANA HATHERLY
for their sewing and cookery skills.

Dorling Kindersley *would like to thank* PATRICIA DEWHURST
for kindly lending props for photography,
and STEVE DOBSON *for his help with photography.*

Border illustrations *by Dorothy Tucker.*